Edition Schott

Alvin Singleton

b.1940

Helga

for Violin, Viola, and Cello

ED 30073

www.schott-music.com

Mainz · London · Madrid · New York · Paris · Prague · Tokyo · Toronto

Commissioned by Charles Siegel for his wife Helga
on the occasion of her 70th birthday

HELGA

for violin, viola, and cello

Alvin Singleton (2003)

2

Violin

Commissioned by Charles Siegel for his wife Helga
on the occasion of her 70th birthday

HELGA

for violin, viola, and cello

Alvin Singleton (2003)

Atlanta, 15 July 2003

Viola

Commissioned by Charles Siegel for his wife Helga
on the occasion of her 70th birthday

HELGA

for violin, viola, and cello

Alvin Singleton (2003)

Atlanta, 15 July 2003

Violoncello

Commissioned by Charles Siegel for his wife Helga
on the occasion of her 70th birthday

HELGA

for violin, viola, and cello

Alvin Singleton (2003)

Atlanta, 15 July 2003

tenuto non. espr.

espr.

1.

2.

Atlanta, 15 July 2003